EYES

HUMAN BODY

Robert James

The Rourke Press, Inc.
Vero Beach, Florida 32964

PHOTO CREDITS
All photos © Kyle Carter

Library of Congress Cataloging-in-Publication Data

James, Robert, 1942-
   Eyes / by Robert James.
     p. cm. — (Human body)
   Includes index.
   Summary: Describes the anatomy of the human eye and includes information on eye problems, eye care, and the eyes of some animals.
    ISBN 1-57103-104-9
    1. Eye—Anatomy—Juvenile literature.   [1. Eye.]
I. Title II. Series: James, Robert, 1942- Human body
QM511.J36 1995
611'.84—dc20   95–18999
                                         CIP
                                         AC

Printed in the USA

TABLE OF CONTENTS

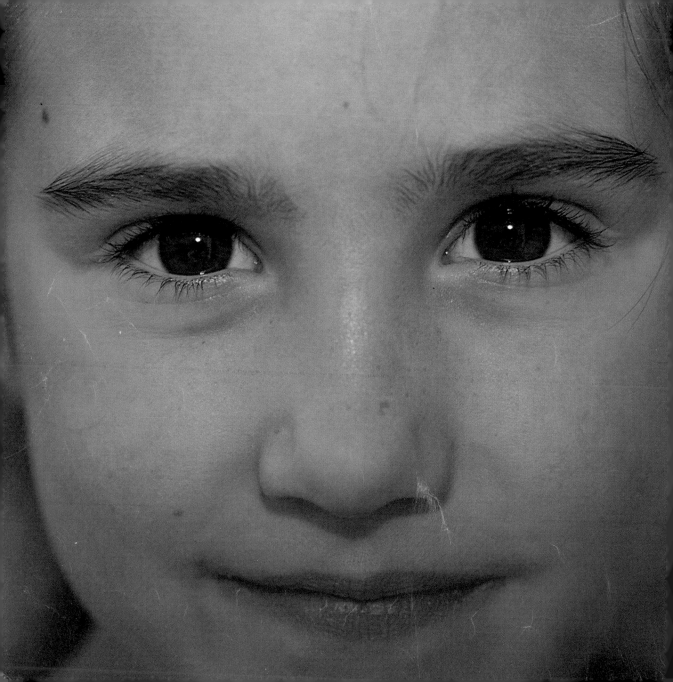

EYES

Eyes are our most important gateway to the world. Eyes are the body organs that help give us our sense of sight.

Our eyes also help shape our looks. Their expression lets other people know what we're thinking or feeling.

We trust our sight, or vision, to tell us much about where we are—and where we're going. Without sight, we would have to depend far more on our other senses.

Eyes tell us where we are, and they tell others a little about what we are thinking or feeling

THE OUTER EYE

The outer eye is the part of the eye that we see when we look at someone or a mirror. We can't see the entire eyeball, of course.

Each eyeball rests in a **socket** (SAH ket) in the skull. The socket is framed by the lower edge of the forehead and cheekbones. That design gives the eye protection.

The eyelid helps protect the front of the eyeball. The eyelid is a thin flap of skin that works like a shade.

The eyelid works like a cover, while the eyelashes help screen the eye from dirt and small objects

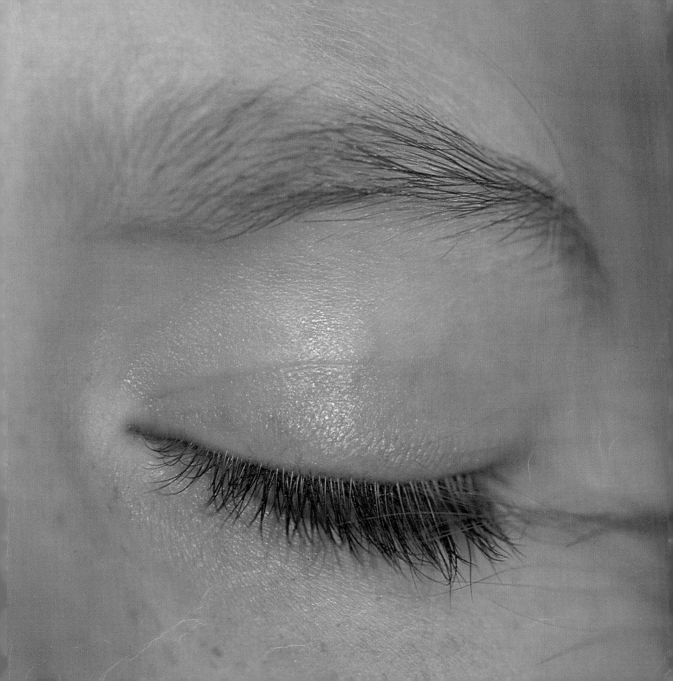

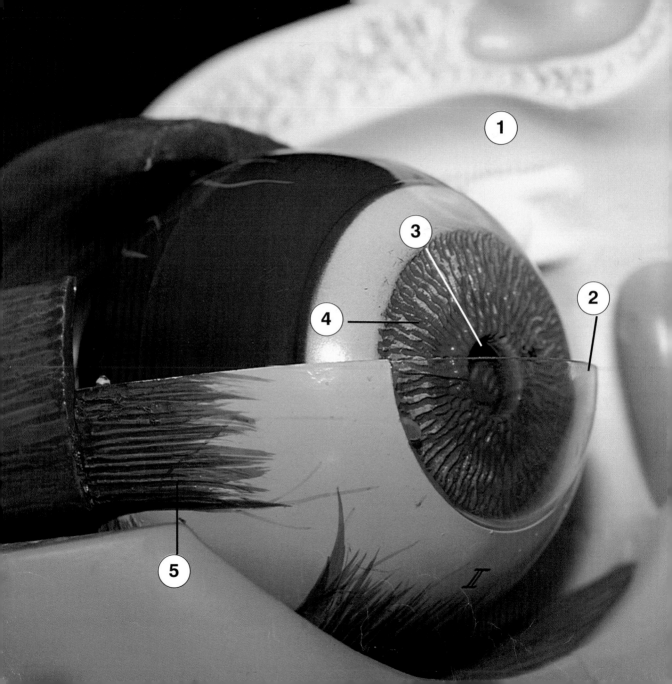

PARTS OF THE EYES

The eye has many important parts that work together. The **cornea** (KOR nee uh), for example, is a clear layer of tissue that covers the **iris** (I riss). The cornea lets rays of light come into the eye.

The iris is the colored part of the eye. At the center of the iris is a round opening called the **pupil** (PU pil). The pupil opens up and closes down with the amount of light. In dim light, the pupil opens.

1. Bone
2. Cornea
3. Pupil
4. Iris
5. Eye muscles

HOW EYES WORK

There are many other parts to the eye. The **retina** (RET in uh) inside the eyeball takes light rays and makes them into electrical signals. These electrical signals are passed to the brain. The brain instantly processes them, and we see the images around us.

The eyes, then, don't see by themselves. They pick up light from objects and send it to the brain. In total darkness, our eyes are useless.

The retina's signals to the brain help people see the images around them— and separate a deadly snake from a harmless bed of leaves

Cat eyes are sharper than human eyes in low light but not in bright daylight

Eyesight opens up a world of color for people

EYE COLOR

Many songs have been written about beautiful eyes—brown, green, black, and blue.

Eye color may affect how we look, but it usually has little to do with how well we see. People with rare pinkish-grey eyes, however, do have poor vision.

Eye color does sometimes determine how sensitive your eyes are to bright light. Dark eyes absorb more light than lighter eyes and are often less sensitive to sunlight.

Brown, black, or blue—the color of eyes has little to do with the eyes' ability to see

EYE PROBLEMS

Like other organs of the body, eyes can be injured, ill, or less than perfect.

A common eye problem is the shape of the eyeball. The eye works best if it is almost perfectly round. Eyeballs, though, are often "out of round."

A slightly long eyeball, for example, causes near-sightedness. A near-sighted person can see close objects clearly—in focus. Distant objects appear fuzzy.

Glasses and contact lenses bring close-up objects into focus for people who are farsighted

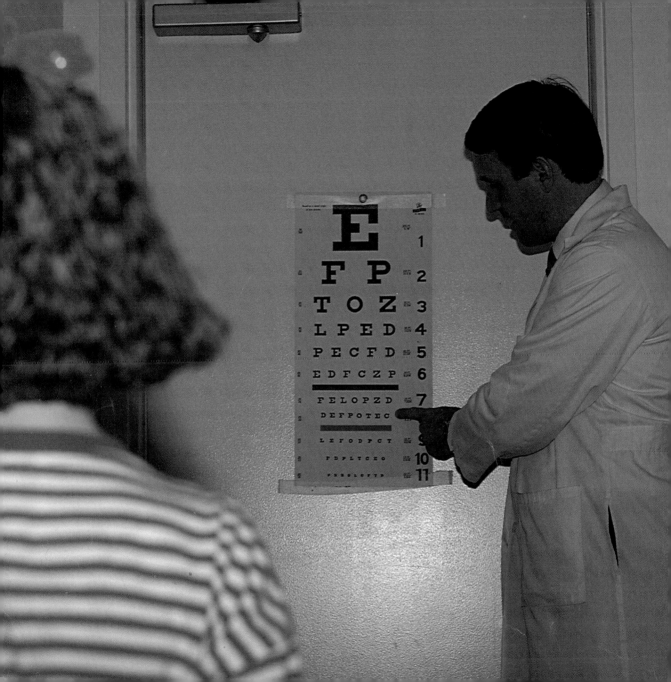

FIXING THE EYES

Many eye problems, like near-sightedness, can be solved with a pair of glasses or contact lenses. Contact lenses work like glasses, but they are very small. Lightweight contact lenses made of plastic actually float on the wetness, or tears, that cover the eye.

Eye doctors check vision, prescribe glasses if they are needed, and check for eye disease, such as **glaucoma** (glaw KO muh). Eye doctors who are **surgeons** (SUR jenz) can operate on eyes.

EYE CARE

One of the best ways to protect eyes is to have them examined every few years by a doctor. If you notice a problem, you should have your eyes examined immediately.

Common eye problems include itching, poor vision (either near or far), double vision, and halos around lights.

You can also protect your eyes by wearing sunglasses on bright days. Wear safety glasses when working with objects that may break apart and fly toward your face.

A built-in clear shield lets the motorcyclist see while protecting his eyes

ANIMAL EYES

Would you trade your eyes for an animal's? Probably not.

Many simple animals can tell light from dark, but they cannot see images. Some other animals see quite well—but they cannot tell one color from another.

Cats have eyes that are sharper than ours in dim light. In daylight, however, our eyes are better.

The best eyes in the animal kingdom may be the eagle's. They're super sharp!

Glossary

cornea (KOR nee uh) — the see-through part of the eyeball that covers the iris and pupil

glaucoma (glaw KO muh) — a disease of the eye that causes gradual loss of vision

iris (I riss) — the colored portion of the eye

pupil (PU pil) — the round opening in the iris of the eye

retina (RET in uh) — a part of the eye that receives images and sends them to the brain

socket (SAH ket) — an opening or hollow that forms a holder for something, such as the eyeball

surgeon (SUR jen) — a doctor who performs operations, or surgery

INDEX